In What Disappears

DATE DUE

In What Disappears

Poems by
John Brandi

White Pine Press • Buffalo, New York

WHITE PINE PRESS
P.O. Box 236, Buffalo, New York 14201

ACKNOWLEDGMENTS: The author is grateful to the editors of the fol-
lowing publications where some of these poems, or earlier versions, have
appeared: *Chelsea, Chokecherries, Fish Drum, Frank* (France), *Celestial Graffiti, Friction,
The Drunken Boat, The Harwood Review, Milk, Natural Bridge, Nexus, Nimrod, Papertiger*
(Australia), *The Texas Observer, Shaman Warriors* (Scotland), *World Poetry* 2002 (India),
New Mexico Poets Anthology: 1960-2000. Special thanks to Holy Cow, La Alameda,
Light & Dust, Yoo-Hoo, Tooth of Time, White Pine, Wingbow, Western Edge,
and the *Kyoto Journal*—publishers who have supported my work over the years.
Finally, a bow of gratitude to Renée Gregorio, my wife and travel companion,
whose patience and help during the many unfoldings and revisions of this man-
uscript were invaluable.

Publication of this book was made possible, in part, by grants from
the National Endowment for the Arts
and with public funds from
the New York State Council on the Arts, a State Agency.

Cover image: Section of a scroll painting by Chang Dai-chien.
From the collection of the author.

Cover design by Jeff Bryan

Printed and bound in the United States of America

First Edition

ISBN 1-893996-63-8

Library of Congress Control Number: 2003100350

Contents

Song of the River

13   Every Road Out is the One Home

14   Deep Motion Inside

16   After Li Ch'ing-chao

17   No Ship Will Ever Take You

18   Yellow Wind on the Java Sea

19   From the Balcony

20   No Superlatives Please

22   What Dagger, What Thirst?

24   Illusion You Spread Deliciously

25   Light Seen Directly

28   Kashi Before Sleep

30   Mekong Nocturne

31   Letter from Kathmandu

32   Song of the Red River

34   Hang Quat Street

36   Perhaps

38   To the Mountain of Perfumed Traces

39   In What Disappears

40   I Reconstruct Her as I Touch

43   Quandary Peak Return

Counterfeit Mirrors

47 Time is a Bullet

48 Porquoi Paris

53 I Almost Started to Say

54 Earthly Silence Overtakes Me

55 You Were Here Again Tonight

56 A Backward Glance

57 In the Sleep of Remembered Dream

60 Under a Passing Comet

62 Words, Engines of Stars

64 Write the Heaven of Now

65 The Waking Mudra of Rapture

Architecture of an Instant

71 After the Hopi Butterfly Dance

72 October, La Luz Trail

74 Love is an Act of Time

75 One for Justin

76 What the Children Say

77 Spinning Forward

78 Arriving after Dark

80 Yagul

81 The Zapotec Way

82 How it Would Be

83 Nalgas Sagradas

84 Architecture of an Instant

Geography Lesson

89   No Rain on the Pass

90   Late Afternoon Over a Bottle of Sake

91   Put It All In

92   My Line of Occupation

94   Geography Lesson

96   No Sister of Mercy

98   Pink Oleander

100   Uncle Joe

103   Confession

106   Final Directions

109   Notes on the Poems

112   The Author

Paso con lentitude
como quien viene de tan lejos
que no espera llegar

I walk slowly
like one who comes from so far
he doesn't expect to arrive

—Jorge Luis Borges

Song of the River

Every Road Out is the One Home

The taste of wood smoke
in high mountain tea. An unfinished path
swept clean by the breeze.

How far out to find the way back?

Five hundred steps
up the pass, three hundred hidden in mist.
Over the top, clouds fill the crags.
Cairns rattle, tumble their stones.

No word for the missing ledge
that carries the feet.
Nothing to mark the way.

Only the moon-washed deck
of love's consent, a few gifts in the trunk,
the path set straight

No matter how crooked
the road I take.

Deep Motion Inside

Across a swinging bridge
held by gorge and sky, jagged peaks
of bannered snow open wide the eye.

Above, through robes of splintered light,
the Great Mother looks down, her silent body dreaming
as far off bells reach me with a piercing sound.

O restless mind that heeds no voice or warning,
here you find things in place, as if at Time's beginning.
All we breathe was exhaled once, as it is again
from gods that live where air is thin.

One crow rides dawn's icy draft
over a bramble gatherer who gives motion
to the morning, her breath hanging
below her as she rises.

O diamond sun above the hazy brink,
my shadow takes the lead
as feet scatter pebbles in your shine.

Motion found and motion lost
to absolute stillness ringed by jetstream cloud,
all one unfathomable, seismographic up and down.

Here, touch this day, clear the hands,
wash the window of the face . . .

This vast, stretching impossibility is reachable.
Beneath these smoky bundled clothes, I feel a body full.
In this uplift of sky-cut rock, another world
brightens from the dark.

Gokyo-ri, Nepal

After Li Ch'ing-chao

The river disappears into haze,
a wet brush swells with oxide and pearl.

How to paint the taste of fine rain
or the small of your back through prismed silk?

Over and over, point the tip.
One after another, tear sheets from the pad.

In twilight, beyond the open door
a slippery path glistens.

Far below, the trail twists.
Hill after hill recedes into mist.

The lamp grows dim, the wind
beats steady on the shutters.

My hand shakes
as it traces your outline on the page.

The wine has spilled, the brush is too far
and I am too close to see.

No Ship Will Ever Take You
Away From Yourself

—Cavafy

Sunrise through glazed reeds.
Abyss washed clean by fathoms of mist.

Halfway around the world I wake
under a cover too thin, finish a poem, fill the pen.

Teapot nods its lid.
High crags shine in warm breeze.

Who is this man working through words
to find stance in the journey?

A foot taps up and down under the table.
A sudden gust turns the page.

Empty, it holds spring sunlight.

Yellow Wind on the Java Sea

Yellow wind ruffles the Java Sea.
Smoke threads island to island on the horizon.

Underwater we glide through coral balconies,
follow needled light into deep ravines.

The body all breath, blue arrows in gold haze,
the mind a courtyard of terraced jade.

Out now, we break through waves,
swim to shore, let the wind dry our skin.

For a long time
in silence we stand, up from under

New to the world,
nothing named.

From the Balcony

Wooden bells echo over terraced fields.
A farmer returns home, closing mud water gates
with his bare foot.

Your face is cool in the candle's extinguished smoke.
A breeze lifts the mosquito net,
adds flowers to your hair.

My body is a blade of light in your sway.
Everything exists, nothing exists.

The ship is burning, your new dress
crumpled on deck.

In the dark, a baby cries, pans rattle,
the rice fulcrum is pounding.

Why muffle our cries,
      why check the rudder
with heaven so near?

No Superlatives Please

There's really not much to it.
If you're a poet, sire delight through what you write.
If a vagabond, fry the fish with its eye pointed up.
And if in Chang Mai, drink heavily of unidentified tea.

I've placed a purple orchid in your hair
over breakfast and helped tie a filigree amulet
around the smooth blue throat under your face.

Today I won't go for my mail. No news from the outside, please.
You've got my shoes, I've got your socks, and together
we're barefoot in Li Po's moonflower shop,
these names and incidents all true.

"And I am glad for everything beyond
the normal and how we choose it," you write,
the back of your leg swollen with a tropical bite.
Call it chance, coincidence, synchronicity. Or what was it
you said about the note Coltrane hit, Stockholm, 1960?

Today I'll caress endlessly
every square centimeter of light rippling
through the air, and not call it something, or look for it
over there, or eat from it in my lap, but forsake the superlative,
be faithful to the shared fidelity of mistaken identities
within the engaged obsession of the moment.

Coomaraswamy called it perpetual
uncalculated life in the present, and Alan Watts,

he wanted to know, does the light in the refrigerator
really go off when you shut the door?

Let's walk to the Alligator Cafe,
catch up on the world's latest evil doings, order wine,
raise our good cholesterol level, sit back and unpsychoanyalyze
those rare blossoms stuck to our heels.

After all, every straight line can be bent
into a circle, a bridge, a rainbow. There is light inside the pockets,
the window of darkness holds a balcony of flowers.
These words let us see out
and in. These stories put us together again.

                                        Puri Lumbung, Bali

What Dagger, What Thirst?

*What is meant by happiness? To live every unhappiness. What is
meant by light? To gaze with undimmed eyes on all darknesses.*
—Nikos Kazantzakis

What histories lie hidden
in these veins and wings, these roamers
walking, peddling and circumcising their young?

What sunrise through the stink of charm,
what beaker of foam, whose flag, what bloodhounds
at the foot of the rainbow?

Where's this kid who comes up to me
in a Jakarta alley with a fetus floating in bottle
for sale from, what's his life?

What's that guy with no arms tying ribbons
around the sky, singing a song of secret beauty
in the middle of day all about?

Where's this woman in lowcut red on the bus
whose thigh wets mine in equatorial heat going?

What bruised arms and walnut skin darkened
with rain eats gravel for a living in the noon ditch
while milk leaks from her left breast?

Who? This Laxmi, this Magdalene, this child
in the back room sewing costumes for the living?

What secret grip undid the knot?
What loosened atrium brought from egg and seed
these coughing sisters of unwed mothers?

Rain fills the vacuum of nirvana. Sparks blow
from the rose in her hair. I am going to the same place
as you on your anonymous bicycle, as you
in your trick of mystery.

The earth is peopled with us. The dogpack
derelict in high towers of glass. I think a thought
in a mirror of canceled evidence, let you suck out
my eyes so I can feel my way through oblivion.

Whose leg under mine
understands the world is a cataract over a perfect eye?
We are clownfish in a reef
while shepherds of crime go about their trade.

This skin inside yours, this sultan's
pavilion, these sweepers of dark streets...
I hear them as we scream, hear the fingers
at the window and my voice like sand.

What is it we call it when we finally remember?
What steeple, what canyon, what lifetime,
whose cry broke the waist of the hourglass?

                                        Jalan Jaksa, Jakarta

Illusion You Spread Deliciously

Low cut Impersonator
of the Dream, I eat you in my sleep.
Suck babylon between my teeth,
make wave and froth in your crease.

I do not fear as you lift,
all hair and flaming smile, to cover
my root and swallow the tree
whose branches hold the sun.

Each time you take me in
I find a new word for light.

You are lavish and wild, you make
strong the body, leave the ego tiny
after you come.

Light Seen Directly

I watched the door close in her face,
the flame inside her go out, and light again
as she returned to the streets.

Marigolds, not money, filled the plastic bowl
at the end of her withered arm. Her scent, ripe like opened earth,
came in rhythms of sweat and ash as I followed her bare heels
to the riverbank, bright and black against the sun.

On the steps beneath a sacred pipal
she sat where years ago I'd seen her, a child of hard bread
whose face opened to the soul. Now she had become woman,
one eye blind, the other consumed in glory.

Between clanging rickshaws
and footslap of eager devotees, she went about
her day, poking through refuse, moving with the easy slide
of mutiny, past the Well of Dharma, to a shrine of lingams
sprinkled with precious oil of coconuts
plucked from the Forest of Bliss.

Here she bowed three times,
blessed her shoulders with fire, planted jasmine
between Laxmi's dark cleaves, and a white hibiscus
on the tongue of Kali.

Once I found her sleeping along the Ganges
in a sandy shore temple, a dead bird, half lice
and tangled hair, half luminous with the water's ripple.

She was of the Shining Ones,
dreaming the world as she slept, and in whose dream
we all sleep: waifs, hypocrites, battered children,
diplomats well fed, graceful women forgetful of death,
acolytes cloaked in rags of prayer —all of us
caught in the Journey's whirling spokes.

Behind her, in the multitude, I stood
amid shouts and banging drums: brides with dancing eyes,
priests holding flames, wild-haired acrobats
bent into impossible liberating shapes.

Adrift in it all, I saw myself aging,
asking for more, while ash from pyres sifted
onto this woman of the streets, her body half hidden
in smoke as she lifted an arm to brush her hair.

Like a magnet, she pulled me,
this luminous woman, matrika of transient names
and forms, to the river, to join others like her
singing in blue gold crimson saris, half submerged
in beams of bouncing sun.

Through prismed mirrors
and countless bodies adrift in prayer, I was carried back
to that first naked yawn, a child in a garden
of color and sound.

In the waters of Kashi, whose light rearranged my name,
I saw myself, new —cleared of loss and limits.
I saw the woman again, saw myself
drawing life from her flame.

Varanasi, India

Kashi Before Sleep

It is never after hours
in Kashi, where sublime mysterium
rises through flaming skulls to shade the zodiac
as I free my light inside your waiting Eye.

It is never the suspected
mantra that begins the poem
as we uncouple from the womb that bears my weight,
but a deeper sublime: the effect of endless turning
through alleys splashed with vermilion
where the quadruple smile of gods quickens the spine
as we approach another auspicious intersection
powdered with gold, wetted with fire
where the dead wait on biers, and women
fling seeds into the air with song.

It does not stop,
this bliss, this ultimate doom losing itself
on the pyre, like the corner of a smile
closing to the wheel of sleep.

We wipe the sword of karma with grief
parading in mistaken victory, kneeling as survivors
of drought and sumptuous lovemaking, feeling
our way up the vertebrae of existence
always reinventing the message.

Like youth crowned
with marigolds, walking the street

in broken flipflops, we spit into dawn's black highway,
become the king who suddenly turns
his face to become the untouchable who nods
her lowered head against the holy banyan
where Mirabai flashed her animal dark
and ran with sparks along the only
road worth traveling.

Kashi, your mouth is a street corner
jammed with beggars, their bowls filled with moonlight
as we lie awake in the soft climb of sleep.
From the balcony, the blinking crown of Durga's palace
invites the imagination into a thin circling motion
that lifts the eyelids with lavish perversions
teasing minute explosions from the skin
as the river ripples into the room
to wash away all questions.

From Kashi there is no coming back,
the longer you stay the shorter grow the shadows
until only a sweet, white ember remains
and blood beats behind the breastplate
like water under stone.

It is never after hours
where grief opens to rapture, and revolution
splits the anchor from its chain
to free the Eye from what is seen.

Mekong Nocturne

River, darklit
among cloud-ragged peaks,
yours is a tough grace mended
with stanzas of fine rain.

Hills rise steep,
the boatman follows no beam,
every passenger is far into sleep.

My pen searches the dark,
my knees fold in, jagged boulders
snag the moon.

I am coming up with flowers
from the sandy fiction of remembrance,
no blame in the way, no doubt
playing games with night's
sweet determination.

Laos, 1998

Letter from Kathmandu

Friends, let us wake with disbelief,
bare our souls, tell our stories, lose our eyes,
become vagrants of the Sea.

Let us seek the heat
of the kernel that feeds in the dark
and step aside of men whose twisted lips
pretend to lead, but are not real
in their pursuit of war.

We've already seen years
of massacre, hydrogen light the night,
children with ruined eyes, tortured by what
no one should ever see.

Let us leave our security,
open our memory, bring flowers
from the storm, write letters that become
sanctuaries, so that we ourselves
may become sanctuaries.

Friends, a dream
runs up to me smiling. I call on you
to see in the dark, to finish
the song inside you.

Song of the Red River

Fields, green with hard labor.
Hoes swinging, water lifted in baskets
one canal to another.

On hillocks, between waving bamboo:
tall ochre houses draped with morning glories,
roof tiles gleaming, courtyards swept clean.

All of it appearing, disappearing
in lacquered drizzle of morning rain.

Two girls now, from behind a levee,
trousers flapping, bicycles balanced with greens.
Pink-cheeked, under conical hats, they gossip
back and forth, trading smiles.

Suddenly, I am dizzy
with what is here, and everything gone before:
broken bodies across the green; rice harvest,
water wells, villages up in flame.

I sit until it passes, letting what is
slowly come back:

Grain bundled in golden fans
at threshing treadles. Old women, willow thin,
over bowls of steaming noodles.

Yesterday, a man who lived
ten years on the Ho Chi Minh Trail, said
"Now the time is to go on." And it does as it has,
without war in the way, go on—

Egrets, a pair of them,
lift into my eyes through gold rain,
snow white in flight.

                                        Song Hong, Viet Nam

Hang Quat Street

there are pink lit halos around plastic Confucist queens
Diesel jeans and fat-bellied Buddhas, a crutch maker
fitting a leg in the rain

there are cyclo drivers wooing stray pedestrians
alleys of ceremonial fans, hammered gongs, blue-chalked
hopscotch squares, and carp in a pond leaving gold calligraphy

there is a child spinning inside a bamboo hula hoop
jars of chocolate the color of white jade
turtles with wings, horses with beaks

trays of crushed garnet, banana flower salad
a sidewalk barber giving a candlelight shave, a seamstress
measuring a man too big for her tape

there are toilets for sale, each with a decal
that says "Liberty According to American Standard"
there are mirror cutters, eel vendors, a scribe at a typewriter
with a pomegranate paperweight

there are low tables of beer, chairs that cannot stand up
old men who cannot sit down, and rain, warm and filigree
over silk and gamblers, cloves and lotus leaves

there are herbs in pyramids that make you dizzy
money for the dead, gold leaf for the brush, aphrodisiacs
paper automobiles

spider mums, sugar cane, cricket cage—

all of these we'll learn to name in a new language
as we sleep, to the baker's trays, to the bread lady's call
to the rooster's voice, to the sneeze

xin chào, pho gà cay quá

dragon fruit, tiger's gate, jade willow
rambutan, rambutan...

Ha Noi, 1999

Perhaps

Perhaps it's the bomb craters
filled with stars after the rain, the raw fix
in the nostrils of tilled fields and wet thatch.

Perhaps it's the bed of the rusted war truck
where the farmer begins his rice seedlings.

Or the television back home
showing war like a movie, but never the widow's
broken teapot painted with falling blossoms.

Perhaps it's the eggplants in the wicker basket
holding dawn through the heat of day,

The carpenter napping under Buddha,
a street vendor offering a persimmon in the mist,
or the baker's lamp flickering before dawn.

Perhaps the mountain path never led
to the bombed temple or the burned clinic,
but to hills of moonlit bamboo where the poet sat.

Perhaps the typhoon washed old battlefields
to sea, and the ancestors' graves bloomed
sky blue with morning glories.

Perhaps it's your eyes, the short dusk, fine rain
turning sidewalk carnations silver, or your hand in mine
on the Bridge of Dawn, your village lit with a sun ray.

Perhaps it was you I was trying to find,
talking to the cyclo driver in the wrong tones.

Perhaps it was the thunderhead
over the ancient script on the red gate
that said "Long Life" —or the wisteria scent

Under the window of the inn
where you shut your eyes, and wanted to sleep
after you told me your name.

Hoi An, Viet Nam

To the Mountain of Perfumed Traces

After climbing 300 steps, past the Goddess
of Mercy, up green switchbacks, then out under blue,
the guide politely asks, "First time, Viet Nam?"

I answer Yes, to the whisking sound
of an old monk sweeping around fallen blossoms
in an ancient temple garden.

Too young to remember the war,
the guide makes jokes about John Wayne, says she saw
how big Americans were, in newsreels, in the jungle
where her father was killed.

In a dim temple cave, she hands me incense.
"For an offering to those gone before."
I hold it, she lights it, our fingers nearly joined.

In the shadows, a tear blurs my eye.
On the way down, the world is veiled in haze.
We stand again at the Goddess of Mercy —silent.

I don't ask who killed her father.
She doesn't ask where I was, Tet, 1968.

Thirty years later, here together,
the American resister, the girl from Thai Binh.

Three bows
to the Goddess of Mercy.

In What Disappears

Sometimes my tongue wanders
among ruins, feels a word lost under the skin,
wants to define the touch, the abyss, the whole
nervous theater as seen from within.

Sometimes my eye exists without me,
and I am carried everywhere at once until the center
is far away and in the blackness, distant as an undiscovered
star, you are closer than you've ever been.

You are my life, my death, my limb.

Like an ocean turned to blood, I find you
in what didn't exist. The moment is carnelian, it runs
from the painting back onto the brush, and I am with you,
completely with you, without me.

Sometimes there is no punctuation
to the land at the end of the point. The surf doesn't pound,
the shore only speaks when we leave. It is you, then,
in me, under and around, who opens into a burning page
and fills the storm with silence.

It is we who write our names
purposely close to the tide's edge
that we may find ourselves in what disappears,
leaving the world to begin, far outside
the painting's frame.

I Reconstruct Her as I Touch

Over the years she's appeared as Parvati,
Guadalupe, Our Lady of Sorrows, Saraswati
and the Virgin of the Swan. She fell asleep on my shoulder
on the bus out of Riobamba, curled up on the concrete
waiting for the Night Express in Allahabad.
She stood in the heat with a cold plate of jasmine
making wreathes at Pashupatinath.

That was her at the rusty spigot
with a plate of tangerines.
She had gold fillings, missing fingers, a bouquet
of thunderbolts between her knees.
She was carved from alabaster, breasts and womb
darkened by the touch of countless mendicants
in the back alleys of Rishikesh. She rode a tiger, stood
on a half moon. Her crown was spiked with narcissus.
Her lacquered arms spread from royal blue
embroidered with kernels of wheat.

Her music was fragrant,
her pendulum warm, her face darkened
by centuries of afternoon sun. She swam in incense,
pondered the catacombs. At the River Krishna she held
an aluminum begging bowl between her eleven toes.
I saw her in Cuzco struggling under a sack of charcoal,
the child orphan in broken flipflops.
She was at the Met wearing glass heels, shouldering
a pet monkey, making eyes at Modigliani.

She was Padmi sorting cockles
on the beach at Mahabalipuram. That was her
in the moonlight on the Zócolo after the earthquake
holding a tiny pair of shoes. She wore a necklace
of butterflies at Jemez. She peddled tickets for the Monkey Chant
from her bicycle in Ubud. She hopped from a Vespa
in fluorescent veils late for a wedding in downtown Quito.
She was Kuan Yin at the modeling agency, the beekeeper's
daughter in the weeds off the road near Zion.

She sat up all night, the angel in white
at the children's psychiatric ward. At Rough Rock
she took first place at the Fancy Dance, in San Ildefonso
she spread blue corn pollen into gold winter light.
She had eyes for me in Aleknagik, sat in the shadows
after serving me flying fish in Quetzaltenango.
I saw her wearing black pearls, Queen of Voodoo
on Telegraph Avenue, I watched her beckon the monsoon
from her spirit house on the South China Sea.

She sold pomegranates
from an upside down umbrella in Mandalay.
Poured cement in Bombay for the New Taj Hotel
at less than 20 cents a day, she poured warm milk
bucket to bucket in the fog in San Cristóbal.

I saw her in Swayambhunath
doing full body prostrations up the hill toward
Buddha's third eye. She placed a grain of rice on her spoon,

bowed to the gods of the Pure Land, topped frosties
at the Creme Queen, knelt on a broken pew in old town,
placed a wreath of fireflies around the Sacred Heart.

She is everywhere and here again tonight.
I see her shift in her seat, hammer a walkway,
scatter a path, send an embrace out of reach.
Her outline is a thirsty ravine, she is time slipped from shadow,
chorus inside a singer. Genesis heralding creator, finish line
inside the runner. Her mane shakes in the eye of the storm.
Her memory opens the phantom gate.

She is carnelian, she is fauve.
She is heliodor, she is jade. Her continent begs
with heated cairns. Her harbor hides the smuggler's ark.
Her violin plays a nuptial feast. She is the wife of no man,
servant of no self. She is a thousand questions inside
the answer, name disappearing
in the gallop of a dream.

She is a luminous presence,
that of someone who's seen the world before
and come again to give it greater meaning.

I reconstruct her as I touch, disappear as she alights.
An island of rhythm spreads over me.
She motions me to her doorway, folds the world
into a paper wing.

Night Express, Bangkok-Hat Yai

42

Quandary Peak Return

It's not done, never com-
pleted. The road twists higher than the mountain.
Water shines from slick rock, a vulture swoops
then knots its dark flare in the sun's eye.

Ponder the skull above a colorless flame,
climb through hissing rain, ink-dashed pine.
Short of breath, retrace your steps into clean, steep cliffs.
Fingers cramp, head feels light.

Is this what you remember?

The inn of good cheer, split by lightning,
windows shut tight. The monastery where the young nun
greeted you with dangling keys, melted into mud,
a boulder through its prayer rags.

Wild azaleas fill the air.
Dark winds erase the mountain.
Forehead beads with perspiration.

This way, that way, which of these forks
was the one up?

A butterfly in a deer print.
Green moss on weathered rafters.
Clouds through the ceiling beams, everything
shape shifting in the rain.

Counterfeit Mirrors

Time Is a Bullet
Derelict in the Mirror

Music through the chimney,
a plate of leftovers in the drafty glow.

In the mirror an old dress hangs
where our bodies once spread in rapture.

It's balmy this winter, raining on Rue St. Julien le Pauve,
shirts on the balconies, dogs at the drainpipes.

I still drive a little car, and sleep
under a quilt of whirling stars.

I wanted to write you, but there's
no longer an address when I open my book.

I won't give you my new name
or reveal what I've learned on the streets

But I can say this, as I receive
her kiss

Water is pounding, pines are bending
and the umbrella she asks for

I open for you.

Pourquoi Paris

You need this exile to take your place in the north wind.
                                                    —Apollinaire

I come to Paris to remember
Orion's path over Apollinaire's grave.
I come to sketch passenger music on Champs Elysées,
a bicycle on the balcony, the moon high like Billie Holiday.
I am here for the blue Odalisque whose jeweled flower
waits under veils of powdered tourmaline.

I come for Victory

I am going to bite the head of a swordfish,
smash gargoyles who guard the heat of flowers,
bring the sun between my branches as the cat licks her plate
and war bleeds from headlines.

I hear my footsteps coming back
        Along the track where no one has been

Today I'll drink flaming cognac at noon, recite Dante
from memory, climb Eiffel's electric tree, descend the pyramid,
see if Mona Lisa has a mustache, find the Korean monk
who paints with a brush tied to his cock.

    I sing of the joy of wandering and the pleasure
            of the wanderer's death

I am in Paris

to discover the lost order of higher Beauty.
In cranes that fly from the metro diva's rush-hour eye.
In fingers held by gravity inside handles of beat-up satchels.
In nipples hard with cold
        and glances ricocheted from speeding windows.
In the shape of endives, and housewives
and tight-jeaned rumps that intrigue the blood.

In sad bag ladies universal to the globe,
in Vincent's delirious sunflower, in the girl from Cirque
du Monde, whose breast is a volcano. In heads bursting
with hope multiplied along
    Metro Les Divines, Metro Bastille
        Metro Du Beau Royaume Dévasté.

Paris, a big red chair where I get drunk
on blackberry tincture poured into colorless champagne
by my lover's mother whose laugh untwists the knots
    from my dread.
Paris, who says "I think, therefore I am not"—my head
is too heavy, my body craves the raw light of the Fauves.

Today, I'll help Botticelli find his miraculous Child
in the hips of a stray cloud, give fifty centimes
    to the tambourine man
at Sacre Coeur, caress the epileptic flower, stroll into
    advancing geometry
of miraculous grins in cubist streets, finish a twenty-course
meal in Cafe Catastrophe with Taramisu, then drink fat page

of electric roulette between French doors
of outer space right inside my head.

Look——

a galloping chauffeur screeches
to miss a giant chandelier (the poet's brain)
beneath a crescent moon over a butcher stall where a madman
in perforated shoes yawns under a commissioned angel.

Paris, whose less-than-perfect measure
reshapes nature with blue gardenias. Paris of diamond aromas
and Sumatran eyes, vague antiquity dusted for fingerprints.
A thousand loves whose sighs congregate in destiny's surprise.
A thousand notebooks opened in the glowing coals
of December cafes. Strange to be here, to smoke, drink,
become part of my own trouble, lick each other's blood
from blue oyster shells, squeeze lemon into chocolate
with people I hardly know.

And what letter cuts like the clang of a bell
  across our memories

Through rose-violet windows on Rue de la Epiphanie,
headless men sort wives from dreams they thought to be.
Moored chess players, their shoes in sawdust, calculate moves
under a spinning Ferris wheel, while I cross Pont Marie
from Ile de la Cité at 4:43 a.m., between a thug
    in baggy trousers

and a Tunisian whose thick finger points to a sleepless man
whose giant accordion has dragged him into a corner,
his dirty ankles pink with cold.

Night of anonymous desire.
Night whose scarf is soaked with myrrh.
Night of the lingering Arabian who sells me a stick
of sugared tobacco printed with a brown gypsy.

Paris, two small breasts that prick my skin.
Paris, the tall Fulani in hammered filigree, rushing
through a riot of headlights with the perfect baguette.
I stand between the legs of a bronze horse, pick up
      a lost glove,
feel heat inside its fur, strike a match, watch the fog dance
like a flare of stained glass.

Paris, I feel a rush
when my hands retreat from your skin, when I talk
in a language I never heard myself speak —for I came
with turquoise and salt, from the rusty debris of America
whose teeth are lost inside a giant yawn.

I smelled your lace, refreshed my skin
with your humid promise. I drank, and am drunk
inside your solar joy. The opera's for free
through the walls of my flat. The bright arrows
of your compass point back at me.

I am here inspecting dreamed things, Paris.
I am your recovery. Your monuments evict me from sentiment.
The dead rouse the morning with hard black eyes.

I hear you waking, Paris.
In the shadows beneath my window,
in the burning letter over my head. I hear you waking.
You are the echo in the abandoned glance
      —your taste gives back my own.

Décembre, *1994*
Av Phillipe Auguste

I Almost Started to Say
the Wild Pleasure

But instead, a dusty tattoo
rode the amber crest of unsure skin
and in the aftershock of what I thought
but never said, I drank the smoke
of night's wing,
        helpless as I wanted to be
beneath the whitewater of your stream,
in the strengthened ember about to flame,
you said
we are free of promise
    we need no names.

Earthly Silence Overtakes Me

The whole laughing
lovesweet gnashing lowerlip just isn't.
I isn't, you isn't, and the we left behind can exhale the wreck.

In so many languages
it's over. Truth begins with terror, beauty has a lisp,
we stumble in the perfection of pleasure.

It never fails, I see you when trying to forget
or find you behind me when I smash a window
just to hear how it sounds.

Now and then we get caught up in need
or disappear precisely when doubt turns a page
from the middle of the book both ways.

Maybe we'll meet in a marketplace,
spread a tablecloth in shifting sand, and break
the unbroken seal——

We who made arson of the hills,
took to the burning forest,
let our hearts grow fierce in the wind.

You Were Here Again Tonight

How easily we could have invented
new names, broken the glass, revealed
the candid child inside the clock.

You of loaded artillery
framed in luminous dust, how perfect
the heat of the wine you refused to drink,

How devastating, how lovely
that mindless panic, that innocent con.

How I wanted you to undress
and become mortal again.

A Backward Glance

It is not the you of long lines.
The windwashed you, the rainblown you of Manhattan,
the exasperated you walking the streets of old Kathmandu.
It is not the you of short lines, of arctic light
splintering below the wing over the Saint Elias Range.
Nor the offshore you rowing backwards into reefs
of solidified language.

It is not this I recall as you.
Not the past participle of mist behind a rainbow.
Nor the predestined verb circling lost cargo underwater
in a village beneath the desert of Mongolia.
But the all at once you, the you of unraveled stockings
with sudden hellos at my afternoon door, the exactly-centered
you, hummingbird at the mouth of a scarlet gilia.
The tequila you in the rain at the opera.
The you of tempered crystal on a shelf by a Chinese novel.
The you of mascara eyes fixed on two birds
in a blizzard whose beaks shine with
dead meat on a highway at night.

It is this that is you.
The you of melancholy proposals and unmarried flings.
The dance-shoe you whose half life privately spirals inward.
The you in a lightning field after sunset, under a cottonwood
whose leaves are the mosaics of Hagia Sophia.
It is this that is you. The warm feather, the rewritten lines,
the print of amaryllis in dark peat, the quarrel over tea,
over the rotation of comets. The catered dinner

eaten with borrowed silverware, the unhooked blouse
beneath a flaming chandelier, the bright veins
of pomegranate, the cold bottles of perfume.

It is this that is you.
The you of frozen shorelines and mountains vibrating
with flowering bamboo. The you of no middle way,
the chameleon you. The Old World you listen to
in coils of deep-sea fossil, in a smoking cobweb,
in the shadow at the center of a dead volcano.
You of undivided highways and disassembled horizons
suspended over blank canyons. The circular landscape whose edges
curl inward, the quick heat inside the throat whose voice
is a clock that does not strike.

It is this that is you.
It is this that wakes somewhere else
up the block down the street to send me on a parallel path
through the reeds into ultraviolet heat, storming cinemas
for a long-distance call.

It is this that is you.
The de Kooning you, the O'Keeffe you
of black iris and headlines wrapped in plastic
on a doorstep in the rain. Phantom you
facing east from Soho, in a trench coat
whose magnetic thread unravels between freedom
and silence. You of wounded love and solitary hiding
whose heart is rain that does not taste.

The you whose book is beside mine.
The you of no punctuation. Hot boulevard you.
Strong arm you, nonchalance you. The you
of no backward glance whose weeks and dates
and seasons have combined neither by chance
nor configuration to make you
nobody else but you.

NYC - Rome - Istanbul

In the Sleep of Remembered Dream

for Allen Ginsberg

This morning, blackbirds chatter,
machines groan, as you look between the spokes
of the thirsty Deliverance Wheel:
   Want more poems?
        Wait till I'm dead.

To celebrate National Poetry Month
you left the world to cultivate holy hallucinations
and *extra brilliant intelligent kindness*
to reconfigure the looks on hardened faces
as you prance from the corporate idol's
pixeled screen, free of footwear
and thought body.

And Blake will sing
from the locomotive's roar,
Treblinka will dance the men of hate
to the remembered breast with sobs of heat.

O watchful, bearded bard
who I last remember in Shakespeare's doorway,
necktie flapping in cubist breeze,
bright star in the Paris night,

May your journey be radiant, may bountiful gusts
liberate you from the shaking wheel.
May you wake in nameless Eternity
where all is well.

Under a Passing Comet

Lovers moaned while the movie rolled.
Silence bled from a knocked-out loser in the ring.
A cat in heat jumped the steps of an old church in sleep.

The human cross looked sad
inside its splintered glass. Under the stars
a beggar's violin opened its wings.

Morning brought flowers from the sun
while people stood in line for gas, butter and psychotherapy.
Newspapers declared the price of meat had risen,
but the price of skin remained the same.

Torture went by the same old name,
dressed to kill in suit and tie.

In a park, between waving trees
not one sneeze undid the tai chi masters
from their calculated frieze.

A gorgeous lady flashed her thighs
speaking aerobic rhythm from 22 showroom tvs
while speed bumps shook assorted rumps
and chess players timed clockwise moves.

Around a corner, came a guy like me
talking to himself under a perfect sky
as Dow Jones took a dive.

For a fact the world was fiction—

Some thought black holes had another side.
Others bragged of their computer's memory, but who
knew how many songs Lightning Hopkins
held beneath his tongue.

Everywhere, successful people applauded careers.
Personalities born from relentless clones peddled themselves
while the rings of Saturn groaned.

Clearly I was alive
in a time when nothing came to an end.
Under the bright, round moon I wiped my eyes.

All of this came to me
in the streets, looking for a friend
while the earth propped its feet on the table
and the lining of my shoes wore thin.

125th & Broadway, NYC, 1997

Words, Engines of Stars

Words pour flames through the house,
flood my eye with fire. I am 200 stories up on a ladder
of pedestrian alphabets.

Words find my secrets, words
can't get enough hours into the day. They bring hands
into the body, steal overtures from the flesh.

Engines of stars, they light cities and bays,
send energy into wheatfields, walk promises
off the promontory.

Electrons of silence, they bend moments
onto the page, summon trivia from wastebaskets,
call bullets from the wind.

In the park, on the bench,
they smolder in spontaneous combustion
as your mouth greets mine.

Words catch our private acts
like the fly on the wall, or lie in our face
to accomplish the delicate task of truth.

I go to bed with words,
speak them to spiders, take into my arms
illicit bouquets of nouns and swaying heat.

O alphabet, this is the voice of a stormy man.

Words in the mirror lost in thought,
each with your own velocity
and fumbled fortune.

Words out of ash and apples
that devour me, caress me, spoil me, flay me,
spare me, save me.

Words that wake from a drought
and bring rain to my limbs,

These words compose me.

Write the Heaven of Now

Write the heaven of now
Write the lost paradise of memory's shrine
Write the teeth of darkness, the white of silence
the star, the thicket, the plum tree

Write a whirlygig, write foreplay
Write to see straight
Write to forget your name

Write no dogma
Write objects beyond thought for little reward
Write the cup and saucer before you

Write a leaf, a fig tree, the table's leg
Write the mirror that prisms the air
and gives back your secret shape.

The Waking Mudra of Rapture

for Ira Cohen

Once again I sit in a seat beside myself
in a tiny cafe along the buried shore of a false sea,
red chile on white plate, Nirvana on tv over the tinseled bar,
Lorca on printed page under a glass of wine.

Outside, the wind stirs micaceous dust
under the moon. Tomorrow is Valentine's, but the window
says FELIZ NAVIDAD. Inside, assorted patrons dine in solitude,
bring flames to cigarettes, some with cloven feet
& eyes half closed, others with untucked shirts & spurs.

The lady behind me taps a glass heel
to her drunken monologue. By the door, a medicine man,
his muddy boots firmly planted in the linoleum,
orders an oversized tea & drinks with the invisible.

I stir my finger into the night,
watch surveyors unroll brittle topography
to a burst of accordions as I look down the green sweater
of the girl scraping plates: her abyss so attractive & deep.

I open a line from Lorca, see him
in youthful prime: bow tie crooked, a smile rising
from the sweet waters of his soul. Above him hovers
the Duende with violin & compass, as he exclaims

Ay, but death awaits me
            before I reach Cordova—

The resonance of those words,
the terrible politics they foretell, the breathtaking eros
built into the terror of the poem's bareback ride—
as if to remind us that any true journey approaches
no expected end, but heaves & jolts at the door
to an arcane world known only to shamans
who've lived & died in the world between.

The sad ship of this cafe.
A stack of Watchtowers flutters like upraised oars
under a whirling ceiling fan. A hoodwinked cowboy plays
with the strings of his bolo tie as the medicine man
takes seven crystals from a deerskin pouch
& configures them under Orion's sleeping light.
The waitress goes about her tables, turquoise jingling,
her perspiration more tantalizing than the cheap perfume
on the woman behind me.

These realities: space imprisoned,
bones of dust & cold heat —they flood my eye
with a dazzle I call the WAKING MUDRA OF RAPTURE:
one that Lorca must have felt
under the huge sky on his way to Cordova,
or Basho, listening to a horse pissing outside the inn
where he lay his transient head,
or a friend in Kashi, who, while watching a poor waif

of a child hauling charcoal for her father,
suddenly saw a jasmine bud fall from her hair
                              & bloom at his feet.

In the remembered dream
we bow to the shivering force
that draws us to the inexplicable jeweled edge
where we squeeze a sonnet from an angel's wing
& peer into a face that stumbles over broken swords
to greet us with arms of smoke.

So it is I come to write, between
the sobbing traveler in the corner who followed
the star of romance & went crazy, & the memory
of an orphan who drowned herself, riding a donkey
into the ocean, its hide catching the sun
in the shape of an upside down cross.

It's nearly 3 a.m. —this place is about to close
just in time to open. Out the window, jagged spires rise
into the moon's yellow eye: tail feathers, they say, of a mythic
bird who fell from the sky before the world was born,
& crashed head first into the sand.

Everywhere, strange beauty—
Black stars, white night, the waitress adrift in slag
of human emotions, looking for quarters, wiping tables,
smiling at Lorca who catches her eye in cigarette haze
between the last few beats of the jukebox.

Why was I born among mirrors?
   I want to live without seeing myself

The waitress tunes the radio,
& does her hair in the mirror to the trial
of a man caught naked in the barn of a small-town
agricultural school with a sheep
dressed in a nightgown.

The medicine man is no longer at his table.
The last cowboy is out the door.
Dawn fills the desert's bowl. The waitress pulls a shade,
all the to better see within. I taste dry light on my tongue,
see a bull sharpening his horns at the gate.
In the corner, a sleeping man drops his arms
into thin air, becomes Houdini undoing himself
from riddled dreams.

This year the vanished comet
that's powdered the heavens with an icy smile
won't circle back on a predictable ellipse,
but will ride its own chorus of wheeling words
through the black jazz of the universe,
to be seen, perhaps, only by the blindfolded horses
at the fence, or from the alchemic tower, where
in our golden throats, the dream circles full.

Year of the Dragon,
Shiprock, New Mexico

Architecture of an Instant

After the Hopi Butterfly Dance

for Renée Gregorio

A star falls through the Great Bear.
Phosphorescence traces your flesh as you bend
with the planet's curve.

This is our pavilion
This is where we join

Breathing blue space
under the wheeling Zodiac, feeling drum chant
in muscle reverberations.

A river of sparks fills your contour
as we paint our bodies ochre, add our breath
to the Milky Way.

I taste your mineral kiss,
trace the desert's flickering edge as you call me in
with delirious gravity.

This is where we bank the fire, scatter pollen
into constellations, invite the rain.

Tonight, we are given decree
by our singular cry.

This is the truth of it,
how far we have come, how long
it has taken to arrive.

October, La Luz Trail

Not much light today as I hike
these cinnamon cliffs and tortoise-shell stone.
Only swirling leaves, wind snapping trees.

Down below, I met a hermit in the firs.
By his smoky odor and huge pack, I knew he'd been
wandering long. Now he'd come through, from the other side,
not tangled in things, but wise.

Had we talked, could he have given
a formula to bring you back? Or would he have screamed:
Bring him back, what foolish act!
for surely your step is lighter now, the curtain opened
to a realm quite opposite ours.

Had I braved today's biting wind,
sat and faced the cliffs, could I have divined
from their terraced weave a message from you?

Bits of difficulty, mad adventure along zigzag trails,
no cluttered thoughts to cloud the mirror?
Perhaps we'd have met, laughingly, bodies free
of the world's vice and flattery.

Today, I find my way through mist and floating spires,
just a little behind you as the storm picks up.
Suddenly, the wind steals my hat,
and spins it away...

In your departure
I feel my own —on the upward path
through a thousand crags   bones chilled
grass turning brittle
        on these tough old hills.

Love is an Act of Time

—Kenneth Rexroth

Night, deep and cold.
I step out of the kitchen into late winter snow,
stars flaring between parting clouds.

For a minute
it all seems clear, this transient life
between who we are and what we believe.

Light years wrap the planet
as we stir the white sauce and test the linguine.
Tonight, we don't discuss or write.

But let the heat of red wine
bring a sudden charge to our bodies
as they pass the table, the plates, the unchopped parsley.

Let dinner wait.
I'll slip a slice of avocado slowly
between your lips.

Let there be only music,
the pine fire glow —books, papers, all of it
in disarray under a table of white iris.

One for Justin

I first met him
in the twilight of a north coast port town.
He was a walking cane of heat, going storefront
to storefront in flapping clothes, elegant as a rooster
amid the drab cathedral of waterfront literati
and well-to-do tourists.

I last saw him
over a table of brown bread, fruit, and wine.
He was a rainbow, ragged, renegade —muffled laughter
leaking from his sleeve, eyebrows arched
with a sly look at the Joker called death
watching from the trees.

In a late sierra afternoon, he stood
with a mischievous smile, leaning on his cane,
the perfect gentleman, palm outstretched
with a single blackberry and a few words, despite
his numbered days, about how extraordinary
to be right where he stood.

And I feel it now, amid
the world's pomp and posturing,
how indeed remarkable —to be alive, every risk
a privilege. In the darkness, the gate is banging.
Spring has come. All the while, the wind
has been opening blossoms.

What the Children Say

That is not a butterfly over my head.
That is a thought I am thinking.

That is not a cloud talking.
That is an eye raining.

That is not a clock.
That is someone who has time for me.

Today I am putting something warm
in my poem.

Tomorrow I won't need water or shade.
Tomorrow I'll have silver feet.

Spinning Forward

for Joaquin Coyote

Naked fields, unrehearsed
in their own glow, tinged with smoke
glinting far below

Music of wind
as the rudder swings 'round
and we slant toward the river

Right pedal down, left pedal
down, tail steady, blade pitched
in horizontal thrust

Son and father, one
luminous nerve ending, a pair
of mallards

Winging below,
the beauty of their shine
and ours

Following the river,
adjusting the lift, climbing higher
than we've ever been

Together,
after so many years, all of it
coming clear.

Rio Grande, May 2000
first ascent in Bell-47 helicopter

Arriving After Dark

We drove and drove,
until the road turned to cobble.
Pine smoke filled the air, and in the morning
there it was: a town with a dazzling tiger up its sleeve.

All bicycles, no cars,
Secret pools and cinnamon trees. A church
with bells ringing unpredictably.

In a small cafe, waiters rose
from sleeping corners to feed the bride
of hand-me-downs.

In the plaza, under purple jacarandas,
marimbas played. Awards were offered
for perfected lingering.

I remember it well—

A town where it was illegal
to be dull. A place up high where stars came to rest
and a fat yellow moon called us to and from
each other's rooms.

Just a little spot, off the map
above the haze and humdrum. Coffee roasting
and vanilla drying in the sun.

A place where women's names
shimmered like islands, and men said Yes
with solar glances.

A town where life opened
on a musical hinge —the ideal life
of chance revelation.

Yagul

for Peter Garland & Esperanza Esquivel

Climbing stone after stone
to meet the rain, I down a slug of mescal,
open my umbrella, lift into clouds, sun at my heels,
shoelaces unraveling into lines of music.

The world is a vertigo island, leafy ravines,
miniature bulls under weeping laurels.

Bells toll, a radio plays.
A guy flops out of a saloon speaking wild
instantaneous poetry. Everything smiles
in its own confused way.

Silent cities, anguished song,
the jaguar crouched in our dreams—
I love the brave, the vulnerable, the specific.

Above the world, anything goes.
Life, the sense of it all leaving,
is what stays.

The Zapotec Way

Stepping off the bus at Tehuantepec,
I'm surrounded by Zapotec ladies who snatch my bag,
place gardenias around my neck, offer glass after glass
of the finest mescal, paint my lips, shower me with gold coins,
lead me to a great monsoon puddle where they smash
the commandments, baptize me with living iguanas,
feed me corn cakes and giant bowls of squash-blossom soup.

Laughing, they tease me with erotic song,
squirts of lime, huge breasts blinking under unruly hair.
These women offer no let up. They drink, carry me to a hammock,
slide watermelon, bananas, peeled mango between my lips.
One rubs my stomach, begs me to ingest a pre-conquest drink:
toasted flower petals frothed with shaved chocolate.
Another sets fire to my straw chastity belt
while furiously rocking me into ecstatic trance-swing
to the tinkle of flashing pendants hanging deep
into her dark cleavage, where the old altar boy of my youth
is forced to bend, lick the salt of her perfume, warm my ears
between huge amber suns, drown away the sexual guilt
of lost boyhood, while struggling to genuflect before
the hundred-proof altar of my about-to-be-buried manhood,
a double death in order to live, a double swig of female breath,
a white-hot charge to shoot me through the Tabernacle doors,
all gold and freshly wet with heat and musk
and stones that lie down to pave the way,
this —the nocturnal mist, sweet assassination
of arms and hands, cool redemption
the Zapotec way.

Hotel Oasis, Tehuantepec

How It Would Be

How would it be not to be?
No brass bands, no iced hibiscus tea,
no sugared mermaid, no roses in Juan Diego's cape.

How would it be?
Without fireworks at noon,
no standing in line for guava ice cream
with the schoolgirls at three, or cold feet at dawn
under Popocatepetl in a second-class dream.

How would it be?
No tug of war between have and have not,
no speed bumps, drag queens, or toothpicks for the teeth.

How would it seem, after 3000 years
not to be eating tamales, to weigh absolutely nothing
after circling your own name,

Your mother dressed in animal skins
and polished obsidian, your father with eyeliner
and flashing mirrors, ready for breakfast
with the Local Chapter of Feathered Iguanas.

How would it be?
Perfectly alien, wandering without toothpaste
or slippers, your cane for a digging stick, your feet
for a compass, the sky perfectly clean
above the Land of the Dead?

Nalgas Sagradas

No voy al paraiso ni al infierno
yo voy directamente al Nalgatorio.
—Efraín Huerta

Like two heaving ships
on two different seas, the great nave
of Eternity nestled between, these buttocks
roll and sway, rise and fall beneath gold-flowered
skirts over embroidered petticoats
in the white surf of day.

Behind them, I ride
each swelling wave, adrift in sways
of robust rhythm, pure marimba,
walking cathedrals of brassy jazz
in whose lavish gardens my eyes sink
like anchors, lose themselves
in spreading heatwaves, until long after day
deep into night, I sweat
wide awake, my insomnia
well deserved.

Architecture of an Instant

Not the broken muffler
on the road to San Mateo, but the green heat
of the girl giving directions.

Not the bruise
of an iguana's bite, but blood
on the bride's sheet at dawn.

Not the Virgin of Sorrows
pierced by swords, but the shrine
to Quetzalcoatl buried beneath her.

Not the smoking volcano
on the 5 o'clock news, but the bull on fire
inside the man with a knife.

Not the mouth at the railing
waiting for communion, but the sound
of a pig outside the door squealing.

Not the sun from polished marble
but dust in the corner
of the beggar's eye.

Not a full moon serenade
but lovemaking
to a chainsaw at noon.

Not the traveller's checks
left on the bus, but the broken clock
in the station where he waits.

Not the view from the stone fortress
but the black daisy
between the jaguar's teeth.

Not the priest blessing a parrot
but the cat waiting its turn
in a cage.

Not the moonlit waves
but the lights of the ambulance
on the water.

Not the couple on the bench kissing
but a child's balloon floating
just above them.

Not Jesus hanging
from his altar, but a dolphin leaping
under the southern cross.

Not what is missing
when the tide is in, or what is there
when the water's out

But who we are
in the sound of the dream
when we wake after sleep.

Geography Lesson

No Rain on the Pass
Yet I'm Drenched

I walk, trails stop.
I stop, the compass spins.

No summit, no drop.
Only endless crags, each with a shadow
darkening the path.

Hard to shake off the world
and keep footing without a track.

Hard to send out a gaze, and find it
still seeking in the afterglow.

What to do when the trail ends
but go on, follow deer tracks
beyond the clouds.

Lost again
where the world begins.

Late Afternoon Over a Bottle of Sake

Blue clouds float
backwards in autumn sky.
Cottonwoods twirl in leaf song.

You open a bottle
of the finest sake. We scan the trees.
"Year after year, the same leaves

Over and over again."
Your hair is white, life is full.
Bodhidharma, Buddy Holly

Memphis Minnie, Chet Baker
now silent in the meditation hall.
Sun stands on its legs,

The broken hoe
has become a morning glory.
You, a funny old guy with lots to say.

Buddha was born from Mara's side.
Christ from a virgin.
Lao Tzu, barefoot, in a falling star.

What do we mean by miracle
I ask. You tell me your roshi told you
"Stand, now sit.

You have just seen a miracle."

Put It All In

for Jacquie Bellon

Fold the armchair, the horseshoe,
the entire datura blossom into your book.
Glue down rust shavings, a snowflake,
the watermark left by the flood.

Paste the lizard tail, a butler's button,
a thousand tons of cliff stones onto the page.
Don't forget the Burmese votive foil, moonlit pollen,
the outrigger's painted eyes, or the wrestler
peeling from the wall.

Collect it, sift it, digest it—

In the hurried tangle of Ko San Road,
behind the unlocked door in Batopilas, on the ferry
to Luang Prabang —open the French wine, the lacquered
shutter, the night-blooming epiphyllum.

On all the rues and sois and calles of the world,
plunge into the feast!

Who said we'd get it all down?
Who ever thought books wouldn't return
to trees, or words to pomegranate seeds?

Night has slipped through the Firefly Gate.
The arctic moon, the paper monkey, the little tin hand
and our own sweet ashes are already laughing
as they sift over Heaven's Lake.

My Line of Occupation

In my line of occupation
I work to light the flame, no time for a job.
Every hour on standby, ready to hasten into the dark
like a surgeon, a burglar, a spy. Now and then I catch a little light.

In the morning, bait the hook, drop into the deep,
bring up a little something wide awake.
In the evening, feed the horse, feed the pen.
Pull the covers from eternity, bed down with Imagination.

In my line of occupation
the phone stays off the hook, the engine runs
best on empty, not too finely tuned.
Otherwise, no bang of unpredictability.

It's overtime all the time.
I must remain wide awake: to speak with snowmelt,
measure dust in the wind, lull strange beasts from memory,
mistake breasts for islands, sort gold from landfills.

There's work to be done, even on Sundays.
Quarries must be drained, eternities reinvented.
Uncertain weight of paper blossoms demands a thermal lift.
Elements of doubt must be delivered to firm believers.

Every verb must be accounted for.
Adjectives sharpened with electricity, stumbles made use of.
I must be less sure the carpet really covers the floor.
Not mistake the walls for boundaries.

Scrap iron, remnants of mislaid rapture,
decent fearful utterances from prisoners, deacons,
beauty queens, waifs —all must find place.

Underweight, practically toothless,
I must bite into everything bankrupt, censored,
obscene, sacrilegious, or suspiciously "decent"
that I've been given to work with.

The materials are here, asking.
I must dig the remains that need to be written.
Excavate, sort the timbers. Carry beams to the summit,
run scaffolding up the structure.

Nothing esoteric, no tricks.
Just lay the mortar, be open. And not too well
prepared. Or all of it, every bit gets away.

Idyllwild, California, 2000

Geography Lesson

We were playing Monopoly on the veranda
when we heard Wayne's brothers, Jacques and Keith,
clomping up the stairs, talking about what they'd do
when they got to the top.

At the door, they stood in white T-shirts,
cigarettes rolled into their sleeves, their sailors' caps
tilted forward in that corky 1950s way.

Wayne begged off. Richard, skinny and quick,
ran through their legs. I was left staring into the game board:
fake money, little wooden houses on Park Place.

Jacques stood behind my chair, his sweat acrid,
sun flashing from his wrist watch. He leaned over,
put his hands on the card table, and trapped my head
between his thick arms.

L'see how Johnny likes the view,
he said to Keith, and clutched me tight, lifting me
over the veranda into the open sky above their Ford
convertible, its top down, two stories below.

I waited to die, and saw from the corner of my eye
the neighborhood tangled in an unfinished puzzle
of tarred rooftops, silver swamp coolers,

Dog Alley, Jim Jeffrey's barn, the cut in the hills
near the planetarium, the huge prop of fake sky

rising from the Warner Brothers lot.

Keith walked up —slow, deliberate, with a grin
predating Elvis. He took a Zippo lighter from his jeans,
held it to my face, and snapped it open with a metallic C L I C K.

Delirium tightened my stomach.
Through the yellow flame, I saw the Sierra Madres
ragged and purple over a moving line of locomotive smoke.
Wayne pleaded with his brothers
            —Aw com' on, he din do nothin.

Below, on the Ford's steering wheel
I caught the glint of Jacques' prized steering knob,
its naked redhead smiling up at me.

Quickly, she was replaced
by a hand at my throat —Ya like it up here?
But no word came from my lips.

A red horse was about to fly over the corner gas station.
A wobbling ventilator squealed on the roof
above the forbidden drugstore that sold dirty books.

Motionless, at the center of a strange disorder,
I was over the edge and suddenly didn't care. Eyes dizzy,
head blank, it was the first time I knew God
had nothing to do with what came next.

No Sister of Mercy

Sister Mary Bernadette did not resemble my mother
nor the Blessed Lady floating above flickering candles
in the church where we used to pray.

She was no barefoot virgin
gracefully dressed in royal blue, tiny stars
glimmering from her cloak.

Sister Mary Bernadette had hair on her chin
and was draped in black, except where dry skin
flaked from her ears and landed on her shoulders.

She was my first teacher, the lady I got left with
from nine to three while mother rolled out dough
and ironed the family's clothes.

Sister Mary Bernadette did not extend her arms
with love over rows of dancing candles
nor part her lips into a generous smile.

She stood erect, arms crossed, and, like
those scary characters in *Tales From the Crypt*,
webs of deeply-etched lines radiated from her pursed lips.

Her wooden rosary rattled loudly as she paced,
barking commands, waiting for answers. Whenever she passed,
a distinct trace, like dirty laundry, lingered above my desk.

Once, on a hot day, I tossed a stale sandwich
from my lunch box into the empty lot behind school.
Sister Mary Bernadette caught me, made me eat it,
sand and peanut butter grinding between my teeth.

Then she gave me a putty knife, took me by the ear
and ordered me to chip dry pigeon droppings
from the steps of the principal's office.

I was in first grade, and I was being educated.
I missed my mother's arm around me teaching me to read,
and the soft face of the Blessed Lady smiling
from her gilded shrine.

I did not believe the unhappy lady
in black costume —Sister Mary Bernadette, with a stick
up her sleeve, going about her routine

Waiting to take it out
on kids like me, quick young foals
who hadn't even lost their first teeth.

Pink Oleander

He comes back to me now
as I drive the freeway out of Vegas, in a rented car
between long dividers of oleander:
the man who jumped me from behind a pink oleander
as I walked home from school one day, third grade.

He was the same guy we used to see from a distance
emptying trash into the school incinerator,
the one with no neck, hired by the nuns
to stab at candy wrappers with a long pointed stick
as we kicked the ball during recess.

After school, we'd hide and watch him
wobble along on his bicycle, a bag of groceries
tied to the handlebars —now he had me in his arms,
he was closer than I had ever seen him, his eyes
watery, like he was going to cry.

I smelled his sweat
as he raised me up and pressed his lips
against my mouth, dropped me to the ground
and disappeared into the pink oleander.

When I got home my mother looked up
at my gray school uniform from a pie crust
she was pinching. How did you get that grass stain
on your pants?

I fell, playing kick ball.

I had to change right away
so she could wash the knee of my trousers.
In the bathroom, with the bar of Sweetheart soap
mother washed my mouth with once for talking back to her,
I scrubbed my lip, skeeping them tight not to catch
the germs of the man who kissed me.

I could see his eyes,
smell his clothes, hear the rusty chain
of his bicycle as I continued to scrub the man away,
and kept thinking: I don't want him to get in trouble.
He has jobs to do for the nuns.

He was all alone, I thought.
He wanted people to like him, so I left it
like that —never said a thing.

Uncle Joe

They strapped him onto the gurney,
straight-jacketed him to his death bed, and that's
the way he was going to go.

Uncle Joe, born with a broken arm,
Italian side of the family.
New Year's Day, 1900.

He had spunk, was in vaudeville, the silents,
Hollywood, the first talkies. Even rode a train
to Cheyenne and took a role with Indians.

He played sax, violin. Loved to dress, act, goof,
do it different. In his spare time he took photographs.
And probably smoked marijuana.

He was a loner, loved solitude, drove
a green Dodge with an undressed angel on the hood.
Then a '51 Ford that earned me 50¢ every time I washed it.

He lived in Hollywood's Fountain Manor,
one of the best. Chandeliers, phone operator, elevator man.
In the stock-market crash, he lost it all.

Forty years in his little room
he overlooked the hills where James Dean fought it out
with a switchblade in *Rebel Without a Cause*.

He was particular about eating.
Oregano but not lemon, peanuts but not chocolate.
And he wouldn't drink ordinary tap water
without letting it sit for exactly seven minutes.

He was also particular about dying.
He wanted to go alone, playing his violin, painting
Hollywood street life from an easel tied to his fire escape.

One Sunday, Uncle Joe failed to show
for a game of rummy. When the family went to check on him,
he was crawling along his apartment floor.

Right where he wanted to be—

But nobody wanted him to go that way,
unable to swallow, raspy with throat cancer. So they stuffed
his clothes into a grocery bag, and drove him
to Hollywood Presbyterian.

Right before he died I was at his side.
Alone, hallucinating, recognizing no one, he was
struggling to undo the straps, pull out the i.v.
Trying any way he could to leave.

When dad arrived, fresh from
Ash Wednesday mass, Uncle Joe looked puzzled:
Whadya do t'get that nick in the head?

Then, as the doctors increased
his morphine, he rolled over and asked:
What came first, chicken or the egg?

I had brought a tape recorder.
His deck of naked-women playing cards.
His hand-tinted photo of a bee in a magnolia blossom.

I mentioned Joe Venutti. Greta Garbo.
Stan Laurel. Sandy Koufax —no reaction, until I said
You know, we're going to get you out.

Sure, he looked at me. We sure are.
Then he curled into the fetal position. And like a movie,
a silent movie, he was done.

Alone. Not at home.
But strapped to a hospital bed. With strangers
looking on. The way he never
wanted to go.

Confession

Bless me father
for I have sinned. I was dull to myself,
dull to my wife, dull to my friends, dull to life
three times last week, and once before confession today.

In trying to behave
I have strayed from the path of imagination,
curiosity, spontaneity, consideration
and wild uncalculated drifts into the impossible.

Bless me father
for I have tried to get every line 'right'
and in so doing have reworked, reworded,
overorganized, and remodified life.

So, have me do penance,
kneel for undetermined hours
eye level with Inspiration, her body meeting
mine with the all-sublime feature of Redemption.

Let me be remarkable—

Let the sun shine
backwards from astounding mirrors
in which I make unsurpassed erotic rotations
in the face of small talk. Let my professional self
wither, my character strengthen.

Please, reinstate my doubt
in the face of those who constantly talk
and think they know, who posture
and bite back at themselves in the courts of law.

Bless me father
for I have failed to swim. I have
been timid at the prow of the sinking ship. I have
not pissed from a bridge nor pinched an ass for forty days.

I have not let my fingers wander
in the dark, nor approached the sweet eye
of a narcissus without expectation. I haven't listened
through a motel room wall, nor triggered a department
store alarm since my last confession.

Father, I know you
are the Great Mother in disguise.
Help me hang the dirty sheets, open my heart
with sabotage, free the enduring
words I want to speak.

Bless me, for I have given you
all the details of my outrageous behavior.
May light strike my body from your thundering tongue,
may the charm be released, the monsoon begin.

In the lucid epiphany,
in the warm conversation of your sea, give me courage
to lose direction, drown in the churning undertow.
With absolute clarity let me surrender.

first day of spring, 2001

Final Directions

Just set me to a match
without the dishonor of pomp,
no undertaker's package plan, readymade wreath
or generic crucifix. A few tears, okay, but please
take it out there with laughter, bottle rockets,
balloons and brass.

Call in the accordions and violins.
Wake those who have gone before me
with enough beer and wine to shake the neighborhood.
No corny speech above open casket to forgive
my crankiness or flatulence, but down-home dancing
under paper flags fluttering above sugar skulls decorated
with assorted names of lovers and martyred poets.

Let fat-bellied Ganesha give his blessing
from a bed of marigolds, and Guadalupe smile darkly
in her shrine of roses. Take my ashes to a cove
where sea otters play and the call of Asia rides a green wave,
where salt foam blows through poppied cliffs,
and sky and water become one
as stars push forward from the dead's domain.

Notes to the Poems

After Li Ch'ing-chao
"Li Ch'ing-chao"—(1084-1151) regarded as China's finest female poet; a distinguished painter and calligrapher as well.

Deep Motion Inside
"the Great Mother"—Mt. Everest; known by Tibetans as *Chomolungma*, Goddess of Wind.
"Gokyo-ri"—summit 13 miles west of Mt. Everest, 17,990 feet.

No Superlatives Please
"Chang Mai"—city in northern Thailand.
"Li Po"—(701-762) China's great Taoist-influenced poet.
"Coltrane" —John Coltrane, sax man, composer, jazz experimentalist; d. 1967
"Coomaraswamy" —Ananda Coomaraswamy, Indian philosopher; d. 1947
"Alan Watts"—philosopher; interpreter of Zen Buddhism; d. 1973

Light Seen Directly
"Laxmi"—Hindu goddess of wealth; popular name for women in India.
"Kali" —*the Black One*; Hindu goddess; a form of Shakti, divine female energy.
"matrika" —Sanskrit, *mother.*
"Kashi"—Sanskrit, *to shine*; ancient name for Varanasi (called Banares under the British); one of India's holiest cities; 500 years old when Buddha arrived.

Kashi Before Sleep
"Mirabai"—b. 1498, a Rajasthan princess who gave up her caste to become a mendicant; along with Kabir, India's greatest devotional poet.
"Durga"—ten-armed Hindu goddess who rides a tiger and slays demons; the fierce aspect of Devi, the Great Mother.

Song of the Red River
"Ho Chi Minh Trail"— secret road on which North Vietnamese infiltrated the south in their campaign to liberate Viet Nam.

To the Mountain of Perfumed Traces
"Tet"—literally, the Vietnamese celebration of the lunar new year; historically, the turning point in the American War in Viet Nam when North Vietnamese launched offensives on dozens of urban centers across the south, and captured the U.S. Embassy in Saigon.

the U.S. Embassy in Saigon..

Hang Quat Street

"Hang Quat"—one of many streets in Ha Noi's Old Quarter, dating back five centuries to when each of thirty-six artisan guilds had their own street. *Hang* means merchandise; *Quat* refers to ceremonial fans. The poem begins on Hang Quat and meanders through the Old Quarter.

"rambutan"—tropical fruit; from Malay, *rambut*, hair, in reference to the bright red cilia on its rind; inside is a large pearly seed with a tart, refreshing flavor.

I Reconstruct Her as I Touch

"Parvati"—Hindu goddess; wife of Shiva; benevolent aspect of Shakti.
"Saraswati"—Hindu goddess of learning, music, painting, poetry.
"Allahabad / Rishikesh"—along with Varanasi, important pilgrimage cities.
"Pashupatinath"—Kathmandu's most important Hindu temple.
"Mahabalipuram"—7th c. South Indian shore temple in Tamil Nadu.
"Aleknagik"—Yupik Eskimo village in Alaska.
"Swayambhunath"—Buddhist/Hindu shrine overlooking Kathmandu; its painted eyes see into the four directions from a gilded tower on a gleaming stupa.

Pourquoi Paris

Italicized lines are from Apollinaire.

In the Sleep of Remembered Dream

Italicized lines are from Allen Ginsberg.
"Treblinka"—Nazi death camp near Warsaw where 265,000 Jews were exterminated.

The Waking Mudra of Rapture

Italicized lines are from Federico García Lorca.

Yagul

"Yagul"—8th c. Zapotec hill temple south of Oaxaca, Mexico.

How It Would Be

"Juan Diego…"—convert to whom the Virgin of Guadalupe appeared (1531) on Cerro Tepeyac, site of an Aztec shrine. She showered roses into Juan Diego's cape as proof of her apparition for doubting authorities.

Architecture of an Instant
"Quetzalcoatl"—Plumed Serpent; god of the Toltec and Aztec pantheons.

Renée Gregorio's poem "Whatever Is" inspired the form in which this poem is written (*The Storm That Tames Us*, La Alameda Press, 1999).

Late Afternoon Over a Bottle of Sake
"Year after year...."—line from Robert Frost.
"Stand, now sit..."—Steve Sanfield quoting Sasaki Roshi.

John Brandi was born in Los Angeles in 1943. After graduating from the University of California at Northridge in 1965, he joined the Peace Corps to work with Andean farmers in their struggle for land titles and civil liberties. While in Ecuador, he began publishing his poetry via the freshly-blooming mimeo revolution, predecessor to the small press movement. Returning to North America, he protested the war in Viet Nam, lived in Mexico, Alaska and the Sierra Nevada, and in 1971 took up permanent residence in New Mexico. He has been awarded residencies by the state arts councils of Alaska, Arkansas, California, Montana, Nevada, New York, and New Mexico—to teach in schools, prisons, and homes for the mentally and physically disabled. An ardent traveler, he has sought source and renewal, dialogue and exchange, with the peoples of Southest Asia, India, the Himalayas, Indonesia,. Mexico, and Cuba. In Bali he served as guide and lecturer for U.S. college students. Currently he is a member of the summer poetry faculty at Idllywild Arts, California. Author of more than thirty-six books of poetry, essays and modern American haiku, he has received fellowships from the National Endowment for the Arts, the Witter Bynner Foundation and the Djerassi Foundation. His paintings and collages are in collections worldwide. He and his wife, Renée Gregorio, live in El Rito, New Mexico.